My Dog's Health & Wellness Records

Pet's Name: _____

Owner's Name: _____

Phone Number: _____

Table of Contents

Vet Information 1

Groomer Information 2

Dog Vaccination Guide 3

Dog Vaccination Chart 4

Monitoring Your Pups Weight 5

Check Ups 6

Bringing You Home 38

Birthday Questions 41

Highlight Reel 80

Notes 84

Primary Vet Information

Name _____

Phone # _____

Mobile _____

Email _____

Address _____

Secondary Vet Information

Name _____

Phone # _____

Mobile _____

Email _____

Address _____

Primary Groomer Information

Name _____

Phone # _____

Mobile _____

Email _____

Address _____

Secondary Groomer Information

Name _____

Phone # _____

Mobile _____

Email _____

Address _____

DOG VACCINATION GUIDE

DOG AGE	RECOMMENDED VACCINATIONS	OPTIONAL VACCINATIONS
6 to 8 weeks	Distemper, Measles Parainfluenza	Bordetella
10 to 12 weeks	DAPP	Coronavirus, Leptospirosis, Bordetella, Lyme Disease
12 to 24 weeks	Rabies	None
14 to 16 weeks	DAPP	Coronavirus, Leptospirosis, Lyme Disease
12 to 16 months	Rabies DAPP	Coronavirus, Leptospirosis, Bordetella, Lyme Disease
Every 1 to 2 years	DAPP	Coronavirus, Leptospirosis, Bordetella, Lyme Disease
Every 1 to 3 years	Rabies (as required by law)	None

DAPP (Distemper, Adenovirus, Parvovirus, Parainfluenza)

DOG VACCINATION CHART

VACCINE	IMMUNIZATION DATE				VETERINARIAN
Distemper					
Measles					
Parainfluenza					
DAPP					
Rabies					
Bordetella					
Coronavirus					
Leptospirosis					
Lyme Disease					

Monitoring Your Pups Weight

A puppy should begin gaining weight from the day they are born. They should gain between 10-15% of its birth weight each day. But a simple rule of thumb is to expect your pup to gain about five ounces (142 grams) per week for small breeds and 2.5 pounds (1.1 kilograms) a week for large breeds.

If your puppy is failing to gain weight at an appropriate pace, they should be checked by a veterinarian. They may be suffering from an underlying intestinal problem, poor nutrition, or even worms or other parasites.

Puppies will normally experience their largest growth spurts at varying points, depending on the breed size. For small breeds, expect growth spurts between birth and eleven weeks of age. Medium size dogs will grow most quickly between birth and sixteen weeks. And large breed dogs tend to have extended growth spurts from birth to 4-5 months.

How much did you weigh when you were:

1 month: _____ 10 months: _____

2 months: _____ 11 months: _____

3 months: _____ 12 months: _____

4 months: _____ 1.5 years: _____

5 months: _____ 2.5 years: _____

6 months: _____ 3 years: _____

7 months: _____ 4 years: _____

8 months: _____ 5 years: _____

9 months: _____ 6 years: _____

1st CHECK UP

Date _____ **Pet's Age** _____ **Weight** _____

Immunizations _____

_____

Notes about medical or dental issues, nutrition, _____

parasite control, behavior, etc. _____

_____

_____

_____

Tests ordered / results _____

_____

_____

Follow up plan _____

_____

_____

_____

Questions, concerns, instructions _____

_____

_____

Cost _____ Next Appointment _____

OBSERVATIONS

Left eye _____

Right eye _____

Left ear _____

Right ear _____

Front left paw _____

Front right paw _____

Back left paw _____

Back right paw _____

Teeth _____

Tail _____

Body _____

Hips _____

Knees _____

Joints _____

Nails _____

Skin _____

Other _____

_____

_____

2nd CHECK UP

Date _____ Pet's Age _____ Weight _____

Immunizations _____

_____

Notes about medical or dental issues, nutrition,_____

parasite control, behavior, etc._____

_____

_____

_____

Tests ordered / results _____

_____

_____

Follow up plan _____

_____

_____

_____

Questions, concerns, instructions _____

_____

_____

Cost _____ Next Appointment _____

OBSERVATIONS

Left eye _____

Right eye _____

Left ear _____

Right ear _____

Front left paw _____

Front right paw _____

Back left paw _____

Back right paw _____

Teeth _____

Tail _____

Body _____

Hips _____

Knees _____

Joints _____

Nails _____

Skin _____

Other _____

_____

_____

3rd CHECK UP

Date _____ Pet's Age _____ Weight _____

Immunizations _____

_____

Notes about medical or dental issues, nutrition, _____

parasite control, behavior, etc. _____

_____

_____

_____

Tests ordered / results _____

_____

_____

Follow up plan _____

_____

_____

_____

Questions, concerns, instructions _____

_____

_____

Cost _____ Next Appointment _____

OBSERVATIONS

Left eye _____

Right eye _____

Left ear _____

Right ear _____

Front left paw _____

Front right paw _____

Back left paw _____

Back right paw _____

Teeth _____

Tail _____

Body _____

Hips _____

Knees _____

Joints _____

Nails _____

Skin _____

Other _____

_____

_____

4th CHECK UP

Date _____ Pet's Age _____ Weight _____

Immunizations _____

_____

Notes about medical or dental issues, nutrition, _____

parasite control, behavior, etc. _____

_____

_____

_____

Tests ordered / results _____

_____

_____

Follow up plan _____

_____

_____

_____

Questions, concerns, instructions _____

_____

_____

Cost _____ Next Appointment _____

OBSERVATIONS

Left eye _____

Right eye _____

Left ear _____

Right ear _____

Front left paw _____

Front right paw _____

Back left paw _____

Back right paw _____

Teeth _____

Tail _____

Body _____

Hips _____

Knees _____

Joints _____

Nails _____

Skin _____

Other _____

_____

_____

5th CHECK UP

Date _____ Pet's Age _____ Weight _____

Immunizations _____

_____

Notes about medical or dental issues, nutrition, _____

parasite control, behavior, etc. _____

_____

_____

_____

Tests ordered / results _____

_____

_____

Follow up plan _____

_____

_____

_____

Questions, concerns, instructions _____

_____

_____

Cost _____ Next Appointment _____

OBSERVATIONS

Left eye _____

Right eye _____

Left ear _____

Right ear _____

Front left paw _____

Front right paw _____

Back left paw _____

Back right paw _____

Teeth _____

Tail _____

Body _____

Hips _____

Knees _____

Joints _____

Nails _____

Skin _____

Other _____

_____

_____

6th CHECK UP

Date _____ Pet's Age _____ Weight _____

Immunizations _____

_____

Notes about medical or dental issues, nutrition, _____

parasite control, behavior, etc. _____

_____

_____

_____

Tests ordered / results _____

_____

_____

Follow up plan _____

_____

_____

_____

Questions, concerns, instructions _____

_____

Cost _____ Next Appointment _____

OBSERVATIONS

Left eye _____

Right eye _____

Left ear _____

Right ear _____

Front left paw _____

Front right paw _____

Back left paw _____

Back right paw _____

Teeth _____

Tail _____

Body _____

Hips _____

Knees _____

Joints _____

Nails _____

Skin _____

Other _____

_____

_____

7th CHECK UP

Date _____ Pet's Age _____ Weight _____

Immunizations _____

_____

Notes about medical or dental issues, nutrition, _____

parasite control, behavior, etc. _____

_____

_____

_____

Tests ordered / results _____

_____

_____

Follow up plan _____

_____

_____

_____

Questions, concerns, instructions _____

_____

_____

Cost _____ Next Appointment _____

OBSERVATIONS

Left eye _____

Right eye _____

Left ear _____

Right ear _____

Front left paw _____

Front right paw _____

Back left paw _____

Back right paw _____

Teeth _____

Tail _____

Body _____

Hips _____

Knees _____

Joints _____

Nails _____

Skin _____

Other _____

_____

_____

8th CHECK UP

Date _____ Pet's Age _____ Weight _____

Immunizations _____

_____

Notes about medical or dental issues, nutrition, _____

parasite control, behavior, etc. _____

_____

_____

_____

Tests ordered / results _____

_____

_____

Follow up plan _____

_____

_____

_____

Questions, concerns, instructions _____

_____

_____

Cost _____ Next Appointment _____

OBSERVATIONS 🐾

Left eye _____

Right eye _____

Left ear _____

Right ear _____

Front left paw _____

Front right paw _____

Back left paw _____

Back right paw _____

Teeth _____

Tail _____

Body _____

Hips _____

Knees _____

Joints _____

Nails _____

Skin _____

Other _____

_____

_____

9th CHECK UP

Date _____ Pet's Age _____ Weight _____

Immunizations _____

_____

Notes about medical or dental issues, nutrition, _____

parasite control, behavior, etc. _____

_____

_____

_____

Tests ordered / results _____

_____

_____

Follow up plan _____

_____

_____

_____

Questions, concerns, instructions _____

_____

_____

Cost _____ Next Appointment _____

OBSERVATIONS

Left eye _____

Right eye _____

Left ear _____

Right ear _____

Front left paw _____

Front right paw _____

Back left paw _____

Back right paw _____

Teeth _____

Tail _____

Body _____

Hips _____

Knees _____

Joints _____

Nails _____

Skin _____

Other _____

_____

_____

10th CHECK UP

Date _____ **Pet's Age** _____ **Weight** _____

Immunizations _____

_____

Notes about medical or dental issues, nutrition, _____

parasite control, behavior, etc. _____

_____

_____

_____

Tests ordered / results _____

_____

_____

Follow up plan _____

_____

_____

_____

Questions, concerns, instructions _____

_____

_____

Cost _____ Next Appointment _____

OBSERVATIONS

Left eye _____

Right eye _____

Left ear _____

Right ear _____

Front left paw _____

Front right paw _____

Back left paw _____

Back right paw _____

Teeth _____

Tail _____

Body _____

Hips _____

Knees _____

Joints _____

Nails _____

Skin _____

Other _____

_____

_____

11th CHECK UP

Date _____ Pet's Age _____ Weight _____

Immunizations _____

_____

Notes about medical or dental issues, nutrition, _____

parasite control, behavior, etc. _____

_____

_____

_____

Tests ordered / results _____

_____

_____

Follow up plan _____

_____

_____

Questions, concerns, instructions _____

_____

Cost _____ Next Appointment _____

OBSERVATIONS

Left eye _____

Right eye _____

Left ear _____

Right ear _____

Front left paw _____

Front right paw _____

Back left paw _____

Back right paw _____

Teeth _____

Tail _____

Body _____

Hips _____

Knees _____

Joints _____

Nails _____

Skin _____

Other _____

_____

_____

12th CHECK UP

Date _____ Pet's Age _____ Weight _____

Immunizations _____

_____

Notes about medical or dental issues, nutrition, _____ parasite control, behavior, etc. _____

_____

_____

Tests ordered / results _____

_____

_____

Follow up plan _____

_____

_____

_____

Questions, concerns, instructions _____

_____

_____

Cost _____ Next Appointment _____

OBSERVATIONS 🐾

Left eye _____

Right eye _____

Left ear _____

Right ear _____

Front left paw _____

Front right paw _____

Back left paw _____

Back right paw _____

Teeth _____

Tail _____

Body _____

Hips _____

Knees _____

Joints _____

Nails _____

Skin _____

Other _____

_____

_____

13th CHECK UP

Date _____ Pet's Age _____ Weight _____

Immunizations _____

_____

Notes about medical or dental issues, nutrition, _____

parasite control, behavior, etc. _____

_____

_____

_____

Tests ordered / results _____

_____

_____

Follow up plan _____

_____

_____

_____

Questions, concerns, instructions _____

_____

_____

Cost _____ Next Appointment _____

OBSERVATIONS

Left eye _____

Right eye _____

Left ear _____

Right ear _____

Front left paw _____

Front right paw _____

Back left paw _____

Back right paw _____

Teeth _____

Tail _____

Body _____

Hips _____

Knees _____

Joints _____

Nails _____

Skin _____

Other _____

_____

_____

14th CHECK UP

Date _____ Pet's Age _____ Weight _____

Immunizations _____

_____

Notes about medical or dental issues, nutrition, _____

parasite control, behavior, etc. _____

_____

_____

_____

Tests ordered / results _____

_____

_____

Follow up plan _____

_____

_____

_____

Questions, concerns, instructions _____

_____

_____

Cost _____ Next Appointment _____

OBSERVATIONS

Left eye _____

Right eye _____

Left ear _____

Right ear _____

Front left paw _____

Front right paw _____

Back left paw _____

Back right paw _____

Teeth _____

Tail _____

Body _____

Hips _____

Knees _____

Joints _____

Nails _____

Skin _____

Other _____

_____

_____

15th CHECK UP

Date _____ Pet's Age _____ Weight _____

Immunizations _____

_____

Notes about medical or dental issues, nutrition, _____

parasite control, behavior, etc. _____

_____

_____

_____

Tests ordered / results _____

_____

_____

Follow up plan _____

_____

_____

_____

Questions, concerns, instructions _____

_____

Cost _____ Next Appointment _____

OBSERVATIONS

Left eye _____

Right eye _____

Left ear _____

Right ear _____

Front left paw _____

Front right paw _____

Back left paw _____

Back right paw _____

Teeth _____

Tail _____

Body _____

Hips _____

Knees _____

Joints _____

Nails _____

Skin _____

Other _____

_____

_____

Our first encounter - how, where, & when did I meet you:

_____
_____
_____

Emotions, reactions and first impressions I had of you:

_____
_____
_____

Your first moments in your new home:

_____
_____

Where did you have your first accident?

_____
_____

Did you come from a pet shop, breeder or somewhere else?

_____
_____

How many were in the litter with you? Were you the runt of the litter? What breed were your parents and did you look more like your Mummy or Daddy?

_____
_____
_____
_____
_____

How did it feel picking you up for the first time, what did you smell like, what did you look like:

How long did it take to think of a name for you and why did I choose this:

Cute, weird or random quirks you had:

Something funny you did when you entered home for the first time:

Date: _____

What your typical day looks like:

_____
_____
_____

A cute/funny/memorable story:

_____
_____
_____

How do you greet me when I come home:

_____
_____

Favorite treat and toy:

_____
_____

Your favorite game to play:

_____
_____

A trick you learned:

_____
_____

Something you don't like:

_____
_____

Things others' say about you:

_____
_____
_____

Mischievous things you get up to:

_____
_____
_____

How you tell me you want something:

_____
_____
_____

Holidays or outings we went on:

_____
_____

Where you sleep / where you're meant to sleep:

_____
_____

Something weird you do:

_____
_____

Date: _____

What your typical day looks like:

_____
_____
_____

A cute/funny/memorable story:

_____
_____
_____

How do you greet me when I come home:

_____
_____

Favorite treat and toy:

_____
_____

Your favorite game to play:

_____
_____

A trick you learned:

_____
_____

Something you don't like:

_____
_____

Things others' say about you:

_____
_____
_____

Mischievous things you get up to:

_____
_____
_____

How you tell me you want something:

_____
_____
_____

Holidays or outings we went on:

_____
_____

Where you sleep / where you're meant to sleep:

_____
_____

Something weird you do:

_____
_____

Date: _____

What your typical day looks like:

A cute/funny/memorable story:

How do you greet me when I come home:

Favorite treat and toy:

Your favorite game to play:

A trick you learned:

Something you don't like:

Things others' say about you:

Mischievous things you get up to:

How you tell me you want something:

Holidays or outings we went on:

Where you sleep / where you're meant to sleep:

Something weird you do:

YEAR FOUR

Date: _____

What your typical day looks like:

_____
_____
_____

A cute/funny/memorable story:

_____
_____
_____

How do you greet me when I come home:

_____
_____

Favorite treat and toy:

_____
_____

Your favorite game to play:

_____
_____

A trick you learned:

_____
_____

Something you don't like:

Things others' say about you:

Mischievous things you get up to:

How you tell me you want something:

Holidays or outings we went on:

Where you sleep / where you're meant to sleep:

Something weird you do:

Date: _____

What your typical day looks like:

A cute/funny/memorable story:

How do you greet me when I come home:

Favorite treat and toy:

Your favorite game to play:

A trick you learned:

Something you don't like:

_____
_____

Things others' say about you:

_____
_____
_____

Mischievous things you get up to:

_____
_____
_____

How you tell me you want something:

_____
_____
_____

Holidays or outings we went on:

_____
_____

Where you sleep / where you're meant to sleep:

_____
_____

Something weird you do:

_____
_____

Date: _____

What your typical day looks like:

_____
_____
_____

A cute/funny/memorable story:

_____
_____
_____

How do you greet me when I come home:

_____
_____

Favorite treat and toy:

_____
_____

Your favorite game to play:

_____
_____

A trick you learned:

_____
_____

Something you don't like:

_____
_____

Things others' say about you:

_____
_____
_____

Mischievous things you get up to:

_____
_____
_____

How you tell me you want something:

_____
_____
_____

Holidays or outings we went on:

_____
_____

Where you sleep / where you're meant to sleep:

_____
_____

Something weird you do:

_____
_____

Date: _____

What your typical day looks like:

_____
_____
_____

A cute/funny/memorable story:

_____
_____
_____

How do you greet me when I come home:

_____
_____

Favorite treat and toy:

_____
_____

Your favorite game to play:

_____
_____

A trick you learned:

_____
_____

Something you don't like:

___

Things others' say about you:

___

Mischievous things you get up to:

___

How you tell me you want something:

___

Holidays or outings we went on:

___

Where you sleep / where you're meant to sleep:

___

Something weird you do:

___

Date: _____

What your typical day looks like:

A cute/funny/memorable story:

How do you greet me when I come home:

Favorite treat and toy:

Your favorite game to play:

A trick you learned:

Something you don't like:

_____
_____

Things others' say about you:

_____
_____
_____

Mischievous things you get up to:

_____
_____
_____

How you tell me you want something:

_____
_____
_____

Holidays or outings we went on:

_____
_____

Where you sleep / where you're meant to sleep:

_____
_____

Something weird you do:

_____
_____

Date: _____

What your typical day looks like:

_____
_____
_____

A cute/funny/memorable story:

_____
_____
_____

How do you greet me when I come home:

_____
_____

Favorite treat and toy:

_____
_____

Your favorite game to play:

_____
_____

A trick you learned:

_____
_____

Something you don't like:
_____
_____

Things others' say about you:
_____
_____
_____

Mischievous things you get up to:
_____
_____
_____

How you tell me you want something:
_____
_____
_____

Holidays or outings we went on:
_____
_____

Where you sleep / where you're meant to sleep:
_____
_____

Something weird you do:
_____
_____

Date: _____

What your typical day looks like:

_____
_____
_____

A cute/funny/memorable story:

_____
_____
_____

How do you greet me when I come home:

_____
_____

Favorite treat and toy:

_____
_____

Your favorite game to play:

_____
_____

A trick you learned:

_____
_____

Something you don't like:

Things others' say about you:

Mischievous things you get up to:

How you tell me you want something:

Holidays or outings we went on:

Where you sleep / where you're meant to sleep:

Something weird you do:

Highlight Reel

Notes

Notes

Notes

Notes

www.ingramcontent.com/pod-product-compliance
Lightning Source LLC
Chambersburg PA
CBHW071751080526
44588CB00013B/2215